REST · REFLECT · RENEW

DSW • HAIKU

BOOK ONE

2018 © Debra Smelik Walling, All Rights Reserved
ISBN 978-0-9962010-7-0

With the exception of the noted quotation all content in this book is created by the author. Author retains soles rights to her contributions to this book, photography and content. No part of this book may be reproduced in any form or format, whether scanned, recorded, distributed, electronic or printed in any manner without prior expressed written consent of the artist-author. Please give courtesy of asking permission, stating the purpose and await approval. Use the Contact Page at www.dswalling.com for your request. Thank you. When made available, the creator of the quote will be changed to reflect such on future printings.

For other books and art by the author, visit www.dswalling.com

HAIKU is a way of letting God know that you are paying attention.

Author Unknown

DSW • HAIKU TABLE OF CONTENTS

Greeting	1	Good News	27
Adapting	2	Grief	28
Anger	3	Harvesting Evil	29
One Gateway to Heaven	4	Healthy Vision	30
Awaiting Death	5	Heated Conversations	31
Awaiting Lunch	6	Heedful	32
Awaken Spirit	7	Herd, Waiting to be Heard	33
Be Prepared	8	Holiday at Marco	34
Beyond Reach	9	Holiday Cheer	35
Call to Wisdom	10	Hostility	36
Cease Resistance	11	Incessant Tide	37
Changing Seasons	12	Identity Crisis	38
Cleans, Purify, Shine	13	Inspirited	39
Dance a Victory Dance	14	It Is Called Grief	40
Decisions	15	Invoke Aspiration	41
Depression	16	Keeping the Faith	42
Distress	17	Let Go	43
Earth Matters	18	Letting Go	44
Ego	19	Liberate Yourself	45
Emma	20	Life	46
End of Old Ways	21	Loosely Said	47
Enduring Hardship	22	Lotus-Eater	48
Enlightenment	23	Ludicrous Behavior	49
Facing Obstacles	24	Mercy	50
Fog Lifted	25	Missing Mom	51
Follow Wisdom	26	Mourning	52

New Beginning	53	Stalemate	81
New Eyes	54	Stop, Look, Listen	82
Northwest Winter	55	Subside	83
No Surprise	56	Surrender	84
One's Bearings	57	Sweet Dreams	85
On Open Water	58	Taboo Subjects	86
On the Boardwalk	59	Testing Patience	87
Optimism Tinged with Realism	60	Thank You Jesus	88
Overtaxed	61	That's The Spirit	89
Pencilicious	62	The Art of Nature	90
Pointing the Finger	63	The Burr Under One's Saddle	91
Reborn	64	The Final Judgement is Near	92
Reconciled	65	Thunder	93
Reconnect with Self	66	Turn Turtle	94
Reflection of One	67	Unflappable	95
Release the Demon	68	Value	96
Removing Blinders	69	Welcome from the Northwest	97
Reconstruction	70	Welcome Spring	98
Regained Consciousness	71	What's the Buzz	99
Release the Gremlin	72	When Turmoil Emerges	100
Rescue Mission	73	The End	101
Roads Traveled	74		
Ruthless	75		
Saying No	76		
Seasonal Disappointments	77		
See Life	78		
Self-Reproach	79		
Silver Jubilee	80		

GREETINGS

A form of traditional Japanese poetry; Haikus are designed to bear the heart and soul of an experience in a short format; written to discuss subjects of the natural world. Not complicated, describing everyday themes and usually offering individuals a new view of common situations.

Haikus are a syllabic poem containing of three lines -- five syllables in the first line, seven in the second line and five syllables in the third.

There is the original Japanese version, an English version and an international version form of writing and creating Haiku. Over the course of time from when Haikus originated the rules, the procedures, the guidelines to construct such have been altered, even changed. Thus, the continuation of some rather strict rules in constructing a Japanese Haiku has lessened.

While sticking with the tradition, I created my own style of Haiku while following the five-seven-five syllable format.

With life as my muse, DSW • HAIKU is ongoing. Each haiku is created from 'what is happening at the moment.' Taking a simple observation with reflective thought to that moment I create an independent poem that proved, at times, somewhat of a challenge following the five-seven-five syllable format. Those challenges offered are my first attempt and contribution to the documented Haiku, that if nothing else provides a gratifying experience for me as I became more mindful of life, of the words that surround me. Might some or all do the same for you.

Debra Smelik Walling
St. Petersburg, Florida

2

revive the spirit
transforming the attitude
to freedom and peace

ADAPTING
Making adjustments with mixed feelings to a new responsibility as caregiver after a death.

distracting ripples
fooled not by the reflection
mirrors do not lie

ANGER
Attempting to find a solution to a disagreement without being distracted by the scoff of egos.

scent of cedar, pine
ascending to mountain high
God, sister and I

ONE GATEWAY TO HEAVEN
Sisterhood observing the view at the peak of our hike, 6800' at Maple's Pass, Washington State.

cleaned, groomed, rotated
oh, a place like no other
love unselfishly

AWAITING DEATH
An 11th hour visit with a Hospice patient, she tells me she is ready .

damp, cool, dark, the morn
enraptured fragrances and
turkey sandwiches

AWAITING LUNCH

Before descending from 6800' there is respite among the wildflowers eating lunch is awe, in silence, listening to the mountain top speak.

ignore an insult
work for good finds happiness
let the truth be told

AWAKEN SPIRIT

Minding little stings and not giving them is the key. Very difficult on this day when a brother who has yet to realize their tease has gotten very, very old.

sun, shine brightly, sun
love keeps no record of wrongs
abolish deceit

BE PREPARED
No matter how calm the waters, like a snake that sheds its skin or a horse of a different color, be prepared for surprises. People are vicious.

moving art, the sky
shape shifting billows of white
perennial awe

BEYOND REACH

Driving over the Howard Frankland Bridge JW and I discuss life taking in the awe as clouds entertain with their ever-changing dance across the vivid blue sky.

past tunnel vision
detach your foot from its path
view peripheral

CALL TO WISDOM

I aim to gently enlighten one who has a mean streak. I first must dispel the darkness from within before moving forward or with the hope to succeed for that matter.

with all we endure
find peace wherever we go
liberate the heart

CEASE RESISTANCE
Reminded of – the fewer desires we have the more faithful we will be to God, to others and to our self.

curious eyes dart
words have lost their importance
touch replaces words

CHANGING SEASONS
A Hospice patient in the process of dying, the family remains speechless. We sit quietly, connected and comforted by touch.

awake, do not dwell
aware of all past mistakes
purpose will be found

CLEAN, PURIFY, SHINE

Asking forgiveness. The past will teach me and mold me for an even better future. That is my aim because on some days it is difficult to move forward.

art speaks when words can't
allow candles to flicker
enjoy the quiet

DANCE A VICTORY DANCE
One thing at a time. Live in the present moment, be mindful and do not forget to dance.

simple the shower
raindrops tick atop my head
to hide or ride

DECISIONS

Summer sun intensified, above a cloudless, periwinkle sky as I ride my bike to the library; before my arrival I get caught in a rain storm.

grayish clouds open
wetness distorts the mirror
blinded by the rain

DEPRESSION
Not a very good day. A wet day and not from the rain.

tears fall, shattered soul
bare birch branches, winter's dress
o, to warm chilled air

DISTRESS

Observing the outside view from the surgical waiting room on this frigid winter day. My thoughts are taken to the winter distress on nature and the patient's distress in pre-op.

fields of waving grass
a shimmering sea of green
the vision of two

EARTH MATTERS

A duo haiku attempt with Brother Paul. After a few golf swings we sit overlooking the driving range enjoying the most glorious day. I received an answer to a prayer, unexpected making the day that much more superb, dazzling, marvelous, positively outstanding.

entangled we are
trapped prey caught in our own web
boastful spider, weave

EGO

Crippled by our own habits we all are. Relatives refuse to look beyond, think beyond, live beyond their way or no way attitude.

> sleepy sleepy dog
> let me go forth in your peace
> end of an era

EMMA
My pain, my thoughts as Emma dog is placed on the stretcher and carried away.

peace, a state of mind
minus the war within one
arise to the joy

END OF OLD WAYS
An awakening for me reminding myself to live as the motto I wrote, "Live, Love and Let it Be!"

attitude of faith
be a prisoner of hope
God is in control

ENDURING HARDSHIP
With thoughts of a family in their great sadness. Their son, murdered December 2009.

mind games taunt spirit
holiday chill awakens
as does marred belly

ENLIGHTENMENT
Having undergone robotic surgery ELK awakens the emotions laden with grief offering, somewhat - a new outlook on life. Amen!

candle flames flicker
the dance is non-forgiving
prepare for the burn

FACING OBSTACLES
Non-forgiving is one in the argument. I sit tight. Tight-lipped and observe while a married couple argue it out.

low, gray clouds hover
wheat entertains as cows graze
mountains soon revealed

FOG LIFTED

Awaiting the view of Mt. Baker hiding behind the morning fog as we ride to another adventure.

pause, breathe in, breathe out
unfold the fleeting moment
notice the moment

FOLLOW WISDOM
Not allowing the current situation to entertain, ah…the reward of being mindful.

surviving with grace
the challenges before her
gray clouds have lifted

GOOD NEWS
ELK receives the news, now cancer free. Thank you Jesus!

darkness in daylight
shadowing, woeful the soul
willfully there will be light

GRIEF
In the beginning stages of my grief grasping for some hope. Missing mom.

private space of some
don contempt and bitterness
mirror never lies

HARVESTING EVIL
Wake up people! Get off of your high horse we are the same.

the glory of hope
the seed of our potential
love the one within

HEALTHY VISION
Do not compromise your Faith and if you do not have it, look for it.

observing danger
restrain the trap to conform
ponder first, thy self

HEATED CONVERSATION

Listening to scoff from BK regarding a Pyrex dish. Biting my tongue to avoid adding my two cents to what might turn into a worse squabble.

senseless minds
take a lesson from the sun
early rise, slow set

HEEDFUL

No one listens mindfully. The sun pays better attention. Chaotic minds race knowing the danger yet moved onward anyway.

door squeaks, eyebrows raise
people come and people go
business as usual

HERD, WAITING TO BE HEARD
With dad at the doctor's office. Waiting room, waiting game.

beyond sea fog mist
lies Naples in the sunshine
sleeping on the beach

HOLIDAY AT MARCO

With ELK and SS traveling further south to find some sunshine on this cold winter Florida day only to find sea fog shielding the resort from the Gulf of Mexico.

passing red and green
the days of ole' time Yule
shuffle with their cane

HOLIDAY CHEER

Christmas Eve day, after a mammogram I observe life around me, count my blessings as I eat lunch when I am greeted by an elder couple in red and green, walking hand in hand, walker to walker.

problems that assail
the clock ticking on the wall
all but mere ego

HOSTILITY

Reminiscing of happy days gone by, a moment of past destruction flashes and I wonder, I pray, when relatives will release the demons they entertain.

buzz, and it's no bee
citrus snow dusting green grasses
still, her voice echoes

INCESSANT TIDE

Difficulty in having to be the one to remove yet another part of mom's passion. Thinking of mom and thanking God that mom's voice continues to echo in her garden. Missing mom.

sunny breezy day
afraid not of my shadow
it's afraid of me

IDENTITY CRISIS
I am angry at myself.

hush, water ripples
cicadas sing in rhythm
morning shadows, dance

INSPIRITED

A very early morning stroll through a Japanese garden in Houston. The moment is glorious - does the humidity and the heat deceive or is it so glorious due to the spirit that follows me as I meander.

saddened souls gather
attempting to sustain hope
the healing journey

IT IS CALLED GRIEF
Visiting with BS, the husband of one who just died only to depart shortly there after upon request. A broken heart wants to be left in the stillness of the moment.

forming barriers?
hello habit energy
awaken presence

INVOKE ASPIRATION
A difficult time participating in a session where I was learning nothing for I already knew what was being taught. Where is the rest in awareness.

darkness, the teacher
patiently wade through the pain
whispering mantra's

KEEPING THE FAITH
Hoping for the best. Hoping one will shift the rudder of their sailboat to see the humor in the journey.

clouds wander up high
limitless the heavens are
feel its freedom - breathe

LET GO
JWW casts his worry and concern to God allowing for great reprieve from the webs that cover his soul.

vehicle of change
earthworm toils the soil
flowers anyone?

LETTING GO
Processing death of everyone and everything. Till the soil to prepare for the new life of a plant so too we must till the soul to prepare for our new life after death - as is the cycle of mom's garden - death happens.

the purpose of pain
expands one's understanding
to end suffering

LIBERATE YOURSELF
One of the greatest discoveries in life.

wisdom, folly one
light, darkness are also one
constant is the chase

LIFE

Families! Juggling the ups and down while living peacefully within, thanks to our Heavenly Father.

it's a day for moms
time to polish the armor
think before you speak

LOOSELY SAID

From experience and what women have shared - having one extend Happy Mother's Day wishes is meaningless, even hurtful when one has no mama or one has a state certified crazy mama or one who will never be a mama. The courage to be honest is difficult so everyone gets the greeting of good intention - please think before you speak.

enlarge your footprints
spirit of the gardener
plant seeds of caring

LOTUS-EATER

BK chooses to stay and complain rather then stay and change - choosing not to deal with practical concerns. I find myself getting annoyed. I pray.

news cripples the mind
unnecessary babble
divides man from beast

LUDICROUS BEHAVIOR

For those that hold a title as a news reporter or journalist I pray for your conscious efforts or lack of. Wake up and look in the mirror.

sustain us, o Lord
strengthen and rescue
redeeming our sins

MERCY
Forgive me Father, I have sinned.

landscapes of the past
endure in the memories
antidote to death

MISSING MOM

ELK and I contemplate Christmas, life, death and surgical results on December 11, 2010 - another day of major significance.

grief crystallizes
a hurricane without wind
awaiting the sun

MOURNING
Accepting the stages of grief and patiently waiting as they run their course.

iris budding iris
awaits patiently to bloom
anticipation

NEW BEGINNING
A telephone conversation with PASJ ends; I pray for him as he struggles and shuffles through grief.

the vine, the branches
sin hinders and entangles
mind no earthly things

NEW EYES
Surrounded by the attitudes, the platitudes, the egotism. Playing it safe and putting my trust in God.

white confetti falls
flurries, I think it is called
kissing green grasses

NORTHWEST WINTER
Outside the bedroom window I watch snowflakes dance with elegance, it has been a very long time.

unpredictable
the wind and the mind of man
prepared is the key

NO SURPRISE
The never ending battle of those who fail to think ahead – my knight in shining armor. Possibly they were never a boy scout… be prepared people because surprises are not always cracked up what they claim to be.

reflections deceive
just like the poisoned apple
the ego will choose?

ONE'S BEARINGS

During a recent trip to visit PASJ and PP - will the decision be to reflect or continue to eat the poisoned apple. Ah, the beauty and power of the Holy Spirit - do I hear an AMEN?

dark water wonder
kissed by the summer breezes
wrapped in sunset light

ON OPEN WATER

Ending the day with relatives - no longer surrounded by the sounds of fear instead the hum of the boat's engine as we sit enjoying nature and the ride.

boat coasts, people toast
breezes ripple the waters
greeted by moonlight

ON THE BOARDWALK

It is a beauteous evening, enjoying the movement of others while chatting with friends on the celebratory evening of a stranger's 'I Do'.

do not sugar coat
the bitterness of ones news
hush, death has its turn

OPTIMISM TINGED WITH REALISM

Terry, a patient - one of the few in my 23 years as a Hospice patient volunteer who actually wanted to talk about her death.

a night of great peace
don't just endure life, enjoy
escape the cocoon

OVERTAXED
Those who follow a crowd usually get lost in it. We need to focus on the steps. I do not change what I do, I change my attitude toward what I do.

pointed is my beak
to glide the vastness of space
blackbird? no, Blackwing

PENCILICIOUS
Gifted a palomino blackwing from the Watkins.

the drowsy flux lands
senses flicker dolefully
brooding the answers

POINTING THE FINGER
Listening with patience while Doodles spitefully tells Noodles what she should and should not be doing before looking inward.

clouded perception
negative emotions creep
let God's love surface

REBORN

We are free if we choose to be. To accept who we are, what we have done or not and trust God. Life is good when Gremlins die.

spirit on the rise
no longer in death's shadow
she grasped the nettle

RECONCILED
The turtle came out of its shell. I no longer feel like I am grieving alone.

dynamics happen
simply love, accept what is
moment by moment

RECONNECT WITH SELF
Best to focus on how we are as one - before we speak and act outward especially toward others.

limitless and free
silent illumination
tells the truth of one

REFLECTION OF ONE
Just me, myself and I as meditate. I now realize I am not as bad as I made myself out to be.

unhealed memory
the dark forces lure within
it is now or never

RELEASE THE DEMON
Imminent, a Hospice patient still struggles with her past and now, her reality.

calming shadows charm
amongst the singing bamboo
listen with your eyes

REMOVING BLINDERS
Sisters leisurely stroll through the lovely Morikami Garden.

found ability
talk about nobility
the sun can now set

RECONSTRUCTION
My thoughts of my life with mom before her death and now, accepting this new life after her death, without mom.

faith expressed by love
our emotions betray us
how awake are you

REGAINED CONSCIOUSNESS
I temporarily fell from the path of Godly ways or was it you?

blinded by anger
take away the heart of stone
and bind up old wounds

RELEASE THE GREMLIN
KSH, remember the past makes us or breaks us.

sharp raindrops free fall
body temperature drops
bathed in beauty, yes?

RESCUE MISSION

90+ degrees. Traveling by bicycle, a long way from home - it begins to rain. Mother Nature extinguishes the heat and quenches my thirst, it is a win, win situation.

nature, our palette
west to east and in between
roads traveled with you

ROADS TRAVELED
Last thought at the end of a 23 day sister road trip, Washington State to Florida.

a common mistake
honoring with lips, not heart
proceed with caution

RUTHLESS
The mouth spews what the heart is full of. Another moment where people neglect to think before they speak.

escape habit once
away from expectations
strength abounds within

SAYING NO
Asked to borrow something and for the first time ever, I said no; mostly due to the attitude, uncalled for bad behavior from BK and for that I am sorry, I cannot.

taxing, the tax line
forgive me Father I have sinned
surviving chaos

SEASONAL DISAPPOINTMENTS

PASS and I tend to his income tax at the local library, patiently waiting our turn doing our best to stay pleasant to the overly annoying, overly merry Andrew taking residence at our table.

madness and folly
oppression under the sun
all is meaningless

SEE LIFE
Watching the world pass by, from road rage to those who trust the media and in between - let go of the madness because we die.

make peace with the past
simmering in resentment
become less obsessed

SELF-REPROACH
While prayer may not change a situation it may change the way you experience it. I am ready, are you?

when blinded by love
eyes become ears and we danced
bound by God's magic

SILVER JUBILEE
Where does time go? Meeting JWW for the first time, 25 years ago today.

unfold the layers
decipher the next chapter
challenge the ego

STALEMATE

Difficult to let go of my own experiences I have created, stumbled upon or thrown at me. Those that caused regret, remorse or embarrassment. Brother let go and let God. Release your past, I pray.

guided by the wind
fearless, soaring like the birds
life is my playmate

STOP, LOOK, LISTEN
Enjoy life, now!

negotiating
with every breath we are free
keep the heart open

SUBSIDE
People are way too tense and way too paranoid. Loosen up people. Life is way too short.

faith empowers hope
moving forward, trusting God
possible because

SURRENDER
Possible when one surrenders their egocentric self.

cold air surrounds me
I'm loving it all night long
nestled in flannel

SWEET DREAMS
Snowflakes continue to dance outside the bedroom window here in Stanwood, Washington.

tear off the bandage
the energy of action
makes a difference

TABOO SUBJECTS

We must remove the bandage to heal, to see the change. To watch the continual patterns of disrespect saddens and I can only hope one day, before it is too late, EKW will realize what is being missed.

embrace in beauty
amidst the silence of self
flight delayed again

TESTING PATIENCE

Stuck onboard an aircraft runway due to lengthy weather delays I listen to the dissatisfaction and annoyance of fellow passengers. What is exchanged between fellow travelers - absurd!.

sounds of early morn
light upon the horizon
with gladness of heart

THANK YOU JESUS
Waking to another day with enthusiasm I tend to my daily worship at sunrise on this early morn.

planted with passion
blossoms bloom beautifully
even after death

THAT'S THE SPIRIT

Believing in the power of Faith, despite death, the one who leaves God's earthly kingdom remains in part, where their passion entertained.

man is quick to speak
nature speaks when it is coaxed
silence speaks volumes

THE ART OF NATURE

lets not waste this day
the greatest gift is your time
love unselfishly

THE BURR UNDER ONE'S SADDLE
Doing something with hesitation while trying to love unselfishly.

closed eyes, shallow breath
a new birth is beginning
death knocked at her door

THE FINAL JUDGEMENT IS NEAR

Surrounded by darkness per request, we sit in silence, holding hands and a Hospice patient who is ready and waiting.

frightened abruptly
sadly, sacred sleep stolen
shouting clouds scud by

THUNDER
Beyond the cozy confines of bed, a nasty storm awakes.

early morn, at night
greeted as I make my way
birds trill rats scurry

TURN TURTLE
Nature and neighbors offer an exciting view while taking a stroll.

death before its time
spirit empty as the womb
trouble adjusting

UNFLAPPABLE
Placenta in hand, on our way to the hospital per doctor's orders.

do come home often
honor your resistances
find love in small deeds

VALUE
One stubborn individual, please quit dwelling on the difficulties and unpleasantness - love who you are with.

frost and sunrise greet
southern eyes too rare the view
a forgotten treat

WELCOME FROM THE NORTHWEST

A change of pace for the next two weeks I exchange my daily view of Florida sunshine and heat for the Washington State sunshine and frost.

unencumbered dance
spiraling, pollen saunters
and we humans sneeze

WELCOME SPRING
From the kitchen window looking out, pollen saunters from the trees like snow from the clouds.

wind carried laughter
whispers of shoreline chatter
clouded skies amuse

WHAT'S THE BUZZ
A walk on the beach in sunny St. Pete.

mighty rivers surge
cleansing sorrows from our grief
redeemed by one's faith

WHEN TURMOIL EMERGES
A family's sorrow continues to ooze after the death of yet another son.

to gaze thoughtfully
a poet's muse
reader, yea or nay?

THE END

With life as my muse, DSW  Haiku continues. Do you like what you read, yes? no?

REST · REFLECT · RENEW

DSW  HAIKU

BOOK ONE

Debra Smelik Walling

www.dswalling.com

www.ingramcontent.com/pod-product-compliance
Lightning Source LLC
Chambersburg PA
CBHW042011150426
43195CB00003B/93